MY FIRST

Vishakha Chauhan

Presentation by *BookLeaf Publishing*

Web: www.bookleafpub.com

E-mail: info@bookleafpub.com

ISBN: 978-93-95784-68-9

First edition 2022

For You!

ACKNOWLEDGEMENT

I'm the kind of person who starts work but always left that incomplete. When I was writing this book I was in dilemma if I could complete this or not, but somehow, I did it. And none of this would have been possible without certain people.

I have to start by thanking the creator of this world Lord Krishna who always guides me through his light. Kim Namjoon, Kim Seokjin, Min Yoongi, Jung Hoseok, Park Jimin, Kim Taehyung, Jeon Jungkook, and BTS, I am eternally grateful to these seven beautiful people who make me begin. When I was lost in the room of darkness, they became my light of hope. *whoosh*

Now, I can't forget the people who are the reason I am in this world of life and death - my parents who didn't really know I was writing this book *surprise for eomma-appa* but their presence alone was enough to encourage me. They were the ones who gave me all I needed and all I would ever need.

And, my friends, whose unwavering support and believe pushed me from the east of suffering to the west of peace.

To all those beautiful people who have a big heart and kind soul, who are givers, who are believers and who make this world worth living.

Finally, to the universe, sky, sun, moon, stars, birds, trees and breeze!

Thank you everyone for playing your role in the making of "My First" and becoming a part of it.

CONTENTS

Somewhere in the Sky

I know he is somewhere in the sky,
I'm talking about the one
who created the life.

When I was lost, he became my guide,
on my darkest days,
he always brings me light.
When I was in my lows,
he took me to the highs,
I never lose hope cause
he's always by my side.

I haven't seen him
but I know he is somewhere in the sky.

He can see me every day,
and can hear everything I say,
he can solve all kinds of hardships,
that's why we all do his worship.

I haven't seen him
but I know he is somewhere in the sky.

Utopia

In my head
there is a Utopic world
I imagine
where we all can
live together,
laugh together,
fall together,
and fly together.

A world where there's
no boundaries,
no racism,
no violence
but only love.

A world where everyone is equal
and choosing yourself is legal.

A world where everyone can be happy,
free from sadness
and can easily show their madness.

A world where people don't get hurt
and only speak the language of comfort.

Humans and Seasons

Humans are the same as seasons,
they come, stay, change and leave.

Starting with the blissful spring,
it comes with blooming flowers
and dancing trees
which turns the whole earth
happy and green,
spring reveals the birth of beings
who can be a king or a queen.

Summer comes next
with a rise in temperature, the smiling sun
and the big shiny days
which infers the human's happy
and bright phase.

When dark clouds start wandering in the sky,
then understand that
the rainy season has arrived,

black cloud portrays
the dark days of human lives
but without them, it's not possible
to grow and survive.

After dark days the season of fall
is on the way
when the green leaves turn red,
when trees shed their leaves,
it indicates the time when a soul leaves the body
of the being.

And the chain of seasons goes on and on!

Dandelions

Dandelions make their debut in the spring
with bright and beautiful yellow blooms,
that allure the birds and bees
and compliments the sky and the moon.
By the passing time the yellow petals get dry
and it brings tears to everyone's eye.

But after a few weeks the dried petals
reveal a white round cotton-like head of seeds
that can be carried by the wind
and can easily "take over" a field.

When the whole world
mourns over dried petals,
the flower bust out with the new sepal.
They all thought it was the end
but no it was the new beautiful start!

Bird in a Cage

She is a bird,
who is trapped in a cage,
living her life, daily in a pain.

She wants to fly
and dance in the sky.
She wants to see the world
with her beautiful eyes.
She wants to see the sun rise
and wants to sing before she dies.
She wants to be free
and sit on the trees.

But,
She is a bird
who is trapped in a cage.

She feels suffocated and restless
living in a cage makes her helpless.
She is struggling with her life,
living it on the edge of a knife.

But,
she has a hope for light that
one day she is gonna fly away in the night.

Away from the world
where she can live like a liberal bird!

Home

And it was the day
when I was travelling alone
for the very first time.

I remember,
I was sitting on the window seat of the train,
looking outside and smelling the rain,
that day everything appeared extra to me,
the moon was more bright,
the sky had more light
and I felt more alive.

It was the feeling
I cannot put in words,
I know I was going far from home.

However,
I felt butterflies in my stomach
and fireflies in my bones.
And in the midst of this all,
I realised that my home could never be
inside of those thick four walls.
But this whole world is my home,
outside of those thick four walls!

The Seven

Moon taught me
to love myself
even though I'm full of flaws.

Sun taught me
to never lose hope
when hung between a rope.

Earth taught me
to love the little lives
cause they also have a right to survive.

Sky taught me
to always be happy
even when the life is full of blues.

Trees taught me
to always grow
even if it takes a long time.

Stars taught me
to always shine
even when it's so dark.

And the universe taught me
to dream big
even if it is impossible.

Dear God

Today I'm very upset
with you because
you are the creator of the universe,
you created so many
beautiful things
you created the sun,
the moon, the plains,
the plateaus and the
clouds silver lining
the beautiful sky,
tall mountains, the trees,
and the oxygen to breathe,
you also created
distinct animals,
insects and birds,
but after creating all these
beautiful things
why did you create the beings?

Thousand Thoughts

It's 12'O clock at night
when nothing seems to be right,
the whole world is quiet and
the moon shines bright.

I'm lying on my bed
staring at the wall,
while waves of thoughts
keep running in my head.

Thought of escaping the home,
far away from the knowns.

Thought of starting my life again
but this time without any pain.

Thought of giving up on my dreams
now feels like a real need.

Thought of getting disappear
cause there is nothing much to see here.

And the chain of thousand thoughts continues…

But then suddenly,
my heart started screaming

as if wants to tell me,
that there is still some hope left within you
you can start everything from new,
if the world can do it, then you can too!

After listening to my heart,
I can see a beam of light
which gives me hope inside
hope to survive,
hope to fight,
and hope to shine bright!

In search of herself

She is a lost girl, who is on voyage
to find herself,
and wants to know who she is.

Sometimes she finds herself as calm as a river,
sometimes she finds herself as stormy as the
wind,
sometimes she finds herself as tangled as an oak
tree,
sometimes she finds herself as a sunflower,
always chasing the sun rays!

Who is she?
A river, wind, an oak tree or a sunflower.
Maybe she is nothing and everything.

Stuck on this island

You are stuck on this island of
worries, pain and hopeless nights.

Each day when the sun comes with yellow light
you try again to make everything right
but you failed each time.

You want to evade the island at any cost
cause you crave freedom the most,
you are trying very hard
to find a way to your home,
on this island you are all alone.

You can't see anything or anyone
all you can see is a sea of pain
from which you just want to run
and live your life again.

But why ain't you seek the help?

Take two stones
and burn the fire to make the smoke,
so that you get discovered by the folks.
I solemnly promise that
somewhere someone will see the smoke
and come to redeem you from all the blues!

You are a Gem

They will tell you
that you are too kind
but you don't have a mind.

They will tell you
that you always live in your head
this thing gonna make you mad.

They will tell you
that you are still a kid
you don't even know how to open a lid.

They will tell you
that you don't have any skill
and one day this will make you fall ill.

But I hope
you will never change yourself for them
because you are truly a gem!

Beliefs

If you think you are beautiful, you are.
If you think you are ugly, you are.
If you think you are strong, you are.
If you think you are weak, you are.
If you think you can do it, you can.
If you think you can't do it, you can't.
If you think you are smart, you are.
If you think you are a fool, you are.
If you think you can win, you can.
If you think you may lose, you already lost.

It's all our beliefs
that shapes us as a person
and we become what we think.

Sign

I'm directionless
always looking for the sign,
a sign that confirms
the path I am walking on is right.

Nevertheless, these signs
are different from what
we see in our daily lives.

Different because these
signs are the signs of cosmos
that always helps me to glow.

If you ever in doubt
ask the universe to
show the sign,
and the universe will
put his heart out
to show you the path that is right.

Now you wonder,
how can you recognise these signs?
So, let me tell you about different signs.
If you see any of these then
understand what you are doing is right.

It's a sign
when the sky starts smiling
It's a sign
when the rainbow appears in the sky
It's a sign
when the birds sing high
It's a sign
when the clouds are moving
It's a sign
when the wind is blowing
It's a sign
when the sky changes its colour
It's a sign
when the night gets darker

All of these are the signs of cosmos!

You

And one day
our paths intertwined.
I still remember the day
it was 27 May,
now it's been almost
1.5 years but
it feels like I've
known you for
several years,
before I met you
I was lost in
the room of dark
and it felt like
everything fell apart
but then one day
you came into my life
out of nowhere with a torch in your hand
just to light up my soul
and fill my empty heart.

Born in Winters

He is born in winters
with enchanting eyes,
pointed nose and boxy smile.

His voice is deeper than the ocean,
his smile compelled the world to stop its motion,
his eyes are darker than a night,
his face glints like moonlight.

He is born in winters
with black fluffy hair,
he looks like a winter bear.

He is full of warmth
which he is spreading from the south to north
there is plenty of love that he holds.
Once you see him, he becomes your home
and with his existence, he makes the whole
world adorn.

He is a poem written by the God
with magic, full of love and words of comfort.

He will love you more than yesterday
and less than tomorrow,
he will remove all your pain and sorrow.

Like the last colour of the rainbow,
He will trust you and love you till the end.

He is born in winters
with purple heart, beautiful soul
and a mind full of different thoughts.

I wish I could

Everything fades away
with time, they say,
but my love
for you increases
inch by inch every day.

You are like the star
in the empty sky,
I can see you each day
but I can't touch you,
I can speak to you
but you can't hear me.

Even though you
are far away,
still, I try to reach you
through different ways
but I know I can't,
all I can do is admire you from far.

However,
sometimes I wish,
I had a Harry Potter broom so that I could fly
to you and tell you
how you always make me happy
when they make me sad,

how you change my world
when everything was blurred,
how you make me begin
when I didn't even know the path
and how difficult it is for me
to love you from afar
when all I want is to
show you my scars.

I will meet you

I will meet you
where the star lands,

I will meet you
where the rainbow ends,

I will meet you
where the sky meets the sea,

I will meet you
where the unicorns can be seen,

I will meet you
where the sun meets the moon,

I will meet you
where the stars appear in the noon,

I will meet you
Even if it takes forever!

What is Love?

Is what we see in movies called love?
Is holding hands while walking called love?
Is talking all the time called love?
Is going on romantic dates called love?

No! That's not love.

Love is never about Romeo and Juliet.
It is always about the sun and moon
million miles apart, can never be together,
still every day they fall for each other,
cause the moon cannot shine without the sun.
Even though they can never meet but still
complete each other.

Art of Kintsugi

Life is a stage
and here we all are the performers.
Performers who enter and
play their roles in the story.

The story has so many ups and downs,
love, hate, happiness and sorrows,
finding and losing people that we borrowed.

But do you know heartbreaks
are the saddest part of the story.

Sometimes,
our heartbreaks are so intense
that it feels like
someone is clawing our heart out
and bringing it up to the throat,
that even breathing
becomes a difficult task.

It feels like it's the end of the story
but trust me it is not
because I believe that
broken can be beautiful too.
And the Japanese art of Kintsugi
is the best example of this.

In Kintsugi,
they repair the broken ceramics with gold
which makes those broken pieces look
even more beautiful than before.

Life is beautiful

One day someone asked me.
What do you like about life?
Why do you repeatedly say that
life is very beautiful
while life is so unfair?
I replied that
I like everything about life
the sun, the stars,
the pain and the scars,
the tall beautiful mountains and trees,
the chirping of birds and dancing leaves,
voice of the rain
that relaxes our pain,
all our struggles, our sorrows
our dreams and our goals
love, heartbreaks
and losing someone we love the most
everything is just so beautiful about life.

How can I?

They can call me stubborn,
for not giving up,
but how can I give up
when I know the
whole universe is with me
and listening all my prayers,
how can I give up
when I strongly believe in myself
that even storm can't break it,
how can I give up
when Jimin told me
to never give upon a dream that
I've been chasing almost all my life,
how can I give up
when I know
if I don't do my best now
I will regret someday,
how can I give up
when I've so many
reasons to not.
And I promise that
I will never give up,
even if it takes thousand lives,
I will never give up
till the sun dies.

I choose myself

They call me heartless
I accept it,
they call me selfish
I accept it,
they call me crazy
I accept it,
they call me delusional
and I accept it.

But one day, they told me
to live according to them,
to do what they want me to do,
to choose their happiness
over the happiness of my heart,
to walk on their path
and that was the day
when I decided to choose myself
over everything and everyone.

I choose my own happiness
over theirs,
I choose to follow my instincts
instead of their opinions,
I choose to listen to my voice of heart
instead of listening to their voice,
I choose to design my own path

rather than walking on theirs,
I choose my dreams
over their pride.

You can call me selfish,
you can call me heartless and crazy,
but I will always choose myself
over everything and everyone!

To my future self

I'm writing this
to the one who is strong,
to the one who can stand still in the storm,
to the one who believes in
the magic of the universe and God,
to the one who is a dreamer,
to the one who is a healer.
I don't know where are you
and what are you doing,
maybe you are in a different place
from where we used to be.
I don't know if you are happy or sad
I don't know if you are still that mad.
But I hope you remember all the promises
that you have made,
I hope you will never give up,
I hope you will achieve all your dreams,
I hope you will always follow the white beam.
Even though you and I are the same person
but still I know you are my better version
I know I can trust you,
now go and live
the world is waiting for you!

End

In the end,
I wish you will
heal from the pain
that you've been
hiding from the world,
I wish that you can
find your happiness
even in the smallest possibilities,
I wish that all
your dreams come
true that you have been
chasing for too long,
I wish you find someone
who will become your
guide when you find
yourself lost in the twilight,
I wish you'll find
your home after
all these sleepless nights,
I wish you'll get a life
that you always wanted
to live.

Love ya!